ALL CHANGE
AT SINGLETON

ALL CHANGE
AT SINGLETON

for

Charlton, Goodwood, East & West Dean

IAN   SERRAILLIER

Phillimore

1979

Published by
PHILLIMORE & CO. LTD.
London and Chichester

Head Office: Shopwyke Hall,
Chichester, Sussex, England

ISBN 0 85033 351 2

Printed in Great Britain by
ST. RICHARD'S PRESS
Chichester, Sussex
and bound by
THE NEWDIGATE PRESS LTD.
at Book House, Dorking, Surrey

List of Illustrations

Frontispiece: Hay cart in Droke Lane

1. Singleton, from Levin Down
2. Singleton Station
3. Singleton Station approach
4. Singleton Tunnel
5. Outside the tunnel today
6 & 7. The first buses
8. Ivy Cottage and Grove Cottages
9. The sheep-wash, June 1909
10. Advertisement for Albert Collins, Cab and Fly proprietor
11. Jack Collins with wagonette
12. Girl with a pram
13. The Post Office, before 1914
14. The signpost by the pond
15. By Singleton pond, about 1905
16. Advertisement for Singleton Stores
17. Tom Reeves
18. Advertisement for Smart and Haslett
19. C. Pennicott, the village shop and Cobbler's Row, about 1910
20. The delivery cart, about 1907
21. Horse-drawn dray near the bridge
22. C. Court, the village shop
23. Horse and Sussex wagon at Swallows Farm, Dial Post
24. Traffic by the bridge
25. The village from the top of the church tower
26. Outside the wheelwright's shop
27. Downview with Gus Mason and family
28. Elizabeth and Tom Staples
29. *The Fox and Hounds*, about 1905
30. Outside the bakery
31. The coach party, a W. I. outing
32. Singleton Church
33. Ladies' cricket in 1747
34. The return match in 1947
35. Singleton school in winter snow
36. Mr. Percy Windo, headmaster
37. Mr. Kibblewhite and his boys
38. Charlton Road, Singleton, about 1903
39. Dr. G. C. Garratt, O.B.E., M.D.
40. Nurse Harding, M.B.E., district nurse
41. A visit from the district nurse
42. Charlie Treagus
43. Margery, Cornelia and Bert Reed
44. Littlewood Farm, about 1902
45. The old coach road
46. The old coach road, a modern photograph
47. Wounded soldiers from Graylingwell Military Hospital
48. Bob Farley
49. Jeff Farley, wounded P. O. W.
50. Jeff Farley and other prisoners
51. Dedication of the War Memorial
52. Maypole dance on the village green
53. Britannia's wagon
54. Charlton, Levin Down and Charlton Forest
55. Charles, 2nd Duke of Richmond
56, 57 & 58. The famous Charlton Hunt
59. The Rape of Chichester, 1815
60. Tom Johnson's cottage
61. A meet at the Kennels, Goodwood
62 & 63. Nos. 30 and 31 Charlton
64 & 65. Charlton sawmill
66. The boy with the penny-farthing
67. Fox Hall, a modern photograph
68 & 69. Meadow Cottage
70. *The Fox*
71. A game of Solo Whist at *The Fox*
72. Edmund Harvey, licensee 1886-7
73. John Kennett, licensee in 1890
74. Young postman probably at Fox Hall
75. Horse and cart postal delivery
76. Mr. Dyer, the postman
77. Road-making in the 1920s
78. Farm group, Charlton
79. Moses Osborne
80. Teddy Wadey
81. Unknown lady

82. Charlton Farmhouse
83. Carriages for Race Week
84. The grandstand
85. Goodwood Races, 31 July 1875
86. The finish, seen from the Trundle
87. The crowd in 1875
88. Winner's horse-shoe
89 & 90. Race Week at the turn of the
    century
91. The Edwardian grandstand
92 & 93. King Edward VII and Queen
    Alexandra in the royal pavilion
94. The race-course from the Trundle
95. Fashionable dresses on the course
96. The Pheasantry at Goodwood
97. Droke Lane
98. Hay cart in Droke Lane, before 1905
99. Old cottage, about 1922
100. An old lady in the porch
101. Road-mending outside *The Star and
    Garter*
102. Advertisement for *The Star and Garter*
103. Harold Kewell and friends
104. Cleaning out the pond, 1905
105. The pond, about 1920
106. A ball game outside Butcher's End
    cottages
107. Behind Butcher's End cottages
108. The vicar with children by the pond
109. Motor-bike and chair in 1905
110. Stacking the bonfire on Court Hill
111. The blacksmith's shop, 1905
112. East Dean Church, about 1900
113. Church choir stalls and font
114. The wedding of Ernest West and Amy
    Norrell in 1905
115. The village band
116. Advertisement for Henry Hopkins
117. Henry Hopkins being visited by Rev.
    Newman in his cottage
118. The vicarage in Rev. Newman's time
119. The vicarage fête and flower show
120. The Church Army mission van
121. The Chapel mission van
122. East Dean Cricket Club, 1885
123. East Dean children
124. Children outside the village school
125. The sheep-wash at Lavant
126. Shepherd Smith
127. Bill Taylor, West Dean shepherd
128. Charlie Waymark, East Dean shepherd
129. Henry Wild, hurdle-maker
130. Horrie Austin
131. Ernie Austin
132. Spar-making at The Stables
133. W. Kennett, rabbit-catcher, in 1908
134. A two-speed ploughing engine at work
135. A threshing outfit
136 & 137. Record crop of Dalmeny oats
138. Threshing machine at work
139. Moses West and his son Richard
140. Henry West
141. The last cart
142. The funeral of the Duke of Richmond
143. An engraving of West Dean Park
144. West Dean Park after alterations in 1893
145. The front hall
146. Some of the guests for Goodwood Week,
    July 1895
147. House party, July 1894
148, 149 & 150. Some signatures in the
    Visitors' Book
151. Amateur theatricals, 9 January 1894
152. A royal house party, 22-24 July 1899
153. Four signatures in the Visitors' Book
154. Ready for the shoot, 1894
155. The Prince of Wales' signature and record
    of shoot, November 1896
156. Shooting in West Dean Park
157. King Alfonso of Spain with attendants
158. King Alfonso's signature
159. Shooting party, 1894
160. Ready for a ride in the governess cart
161. Guests from West Dean Park at
    Goodwood, 25-30 July 1898
162. The wagonette
163. An afternoon under the trees, July 1894
164 & 165. Edward James, Presentation of
    Gold Plate
166. Edward James in the Oak Hall
167. Outside West Dean shop
168. West Dean shop, World War 2
169. George Penny
170. Jack Daniel and H. P. Renwick
171. In *The Selsey Arms*, West Dean
172. Keith Phillips, Algy and George
    Lillywhite
173. Roger Champion
174. Pendean Farmhouse
175. Singleton pond in the 1960s

Introduction

This book is a personal view of the Singleton district in West Sussex as it used to be. Many of the photographs are from family collections. A few had been damaged or even thrown away and had to be rescued and restored. Others came from a box of glass plates found in Charlton. I have also included some postcards, engravings, drawings and old advertisements, as well as photographs of some Goodwood paintings from the more distant past.

I am very grateful to all those who have kindly told me about earlier days, lent photographs or other material and helped in a variety of ways. Most of the information here comes from people rather than books. If there are any inaccuracies, or any omissions in the list of acknowledgements, I hope that I may be treated with true Sussex forbearance.

I. S.

Acknowledgements

I am very grateful to the following for all their help: Mr. A. T. Appleton; Mr. J. R. Armstrong; Mrs. G. Atkinson; Mr. H. Austin; Rev. J. H. Bishop; Chichester Photographic Co.; Mr. C. Conway; Mr. E. Court; Mr. M. Cutten; Mr. A. Dadley; Mrs. M. Dorrington; Mr. C. Edgington; Mr. J. Elliott; the late Mr. J. Farley; Mrs. J. R. A. Fogden; Mr. Christopher Fry; Mrs. A. H. Geddes; the Goodwood Estate Co.; Dr. and Mrs. Robert Gittings; Sister Grace Katharine CHN; Mr. R. Harmer; C. Howard & Son; Mr. M. Heymann; Edward F. W. James and the Trustees of the Edward James Foundation; Mr. and Mrs. John Kent; Mrs. M. Johnson; Mrs. B. Kerridge; Mrs. D. Knight; Mrs. N. Laishley; Mrs. F. E. Lanchester; Mrs. E. Layton; Mr. A. Lillywhite; Mr. A. Long; Mr. and Mrs. P. Norrell; Mr. Noel Osborne; Mr. R. Pailthorpe; my daughter, Anne Parker; Mr. V. Parsons; Mrs. J. Pearce; Mr. D. G. Penny; Portsmouth and Sunderland Newspapers; Mr. C. Pratt; Mr. Bernard Price; Mrs. E. Reeves; Mrs. E. Saulsbury; my wife Anne and our son Andrew Serraillier; Dr. Martin Shaw; Mrs. H. Smith; the late Mr. R. Staples; Mr. S. Staples; Mr. F. L. Stevens; Mrs. E. Strudwick; Mr. W. Taylor; Mrs. D. Trayes; Mr. M. Wall; Mrs. H. Webb; Mr. C. Wells; Mr. L. West; the late Mrs. M. Whitmarsh; Dr. I. D. Willatt; Mr. C. H. S. Zeuner; Singleton and East Dean Women's Institute and their collection 'Our Villages within Living Memory, 1958'.

I have also found the following publications very helpful: Anon., *The Historicall Account of the Rise and Progress of the Charlton Congress,* (poem of 1737); David Hunn, *Goodwood,* Davis-Poynter 1975; *The Duke and His Friends,* the life and letters of the second Duke of Richmond, by the Earl of March, later the eighth Duke of Richmond and Gordon, 1911; Ian Nairn and Nikolaus Pevsner, *Buildings of England,* Penguin Books; M. S. Warren, 'Entertaining their Majesties', *The Lady's Realm* 1904–1905, Arrow Books 1972.

Singleton

Amidst the South Saxonian hills, there runs
a verdant fruitful vale, in which, at once
four small, and pretty villages are seen;
Eastden the one, does first supply the spring,
whence milky Lavant, takes his future course;
Charleton, the next, the beauty of the four,
from twenty chalky rills, fresh vigour adds,
then swiftly on, his force redoubled, he
thro' all the meads, to Singletown does glide;
more strength, he there received, at Westden next,
his last recruit he makes, then boldly runs,
till less confin'd, he wider spreads his fame,
and passing Lavant, there he takes his name.

from *The Historicall Account of the Rise and Progress of the Charlton Congress,* a long anonymous
poem about the early history of the Charlton Hunt. The Duke of Richmond wrote on the fly-leaf:
'This was brought to me by a Porter in the beginning of February, 1737. R.'

1. Singleton, from Levin Down, about 1907.

2. (*opposite above*) Singleton Station, London, Brighton and South Coast Railway, 1880-1958 (last passenger train 1935). Trains were punctual and there was at least one good train a day from Chichester to Victoria. Every morning two school trains — with girls bound for Chichester High School and boys on their way to Midhurst Grammar School — met at Singleton. After the Midhurst train started, a favourite game with the boys was to throw someone's cap out of the window. The owner had to jump out, pick it up, run along beside the train, then jump in again. The occasional day excursion from Singleton (dep. 8 a.m.) to Victoria (dep. midnight), 2/6d return, was very popular, and most of the village went. Once an elderly passenger, we are told, was so enchanted by Victoria Station that he never came back. By the early 19 the platforms at Singleton were derelict. Trees waved their branches where royalty, as well as humbler folk, once used to alight.

(*below*) Singleton Station approach, soon after the beech trees were planted. The stationmaster lived in the building
n the right. The waiting room, with its stained glass windows and fine Canadian pinewood, was used by King Edward
II when he went to the races at Goodwood or to stay at West Dean Park. It was said to be one of the most comfortable
England. In the building on the far left were lavatories and a barber's shop.

The railway staff of seven are lined up in front of the station entrance. Until World War I there were never fewer than
ve. Afterwards, as the buses took over, the number was gradually reduced. Finally, Dorman the signalman took on the
obs of booking clerk, porter and stationmaster too. It would be interesting to know how much he was paid in this
ultiple position.

Since 1972 Ian and Andrew Paget have leased the station buildings from the West Dean Estate and planted a vineyard
n the hill behind — the first vineyard in the district since Roman times. Their Chilsdown white wine is produced in the
ormer waiting room and even bottled on the premises. The building that was once used for lavatories is now a conven-
nt wine store.

4. Singleton Tunnel, 741 yards long, above Cucumber Farm. This photograph and the previous two were taken by the engineer.

5. Outside the tunnel today.

7. The first buses were small red single-deckers and Mr. W. G. Dowle, a Chilgrove farmer, started a regular service (four ...es daily) from Chichester to East Dean via Lavant, West Dean and Singleton. Mr. Westbrook, the small man in a cap, and ... Carpenter of West Dean were the drivers. If signalled they would stop for anyone — except train passengers alighting at ...gleton station. After some years the buses won the battle against the trains, and Mr. Dowle sold out to the Southdown ...npany, of which he became a director.

8. Ivy Cottage (far left) and Grove Cottages. On the left of the road is the River Lavant, which rises in Charlton Fores and meanders through water-meadows and villages on its way to Chichester Harbour. (The word 'lavant' means a strear that flows intermittently). Before the sheep-washing the watergate half way to West Dean and the stoppers (on the left were closed to build up the water, and the road was fenced off with hurdles to hold back the sheep.

9. The sheep-wash, June 1909. Most local shepherds used this she wash in time to clean the wool bef shearing. Up the lane past Ivy Cott the sheep were penned in batches twenty or so, then tossed into the river, scrubbed and ducked and released to swim downstream. The long pole the old shepherd is using had an iron ring on the end which was slipped over the sheep's head help bring it ashore. Afterwards th farmer treated the shepherds to be at *The Horse and Groom.* There w no more sheep-washing here after World War 1. William Staples, sex and clerk, records that in 1903 a child was drowned here.

Albert Collins, Cab and Fly proprietor. From T. Pike's *Directory* for 1886-7, District Blue Book with Historical Notes for the South-West.

ALBERT COLLINS,
CAB & FLY PROPRIETOR,
SINGLETON.

Close and Open Carriages on Hire by the Day or Hour.

TRAINS MET BY APPOINTMENT.

Jack Collins with wagonette outside Grove Cottages at the turn of the century. He lived with his father Henry, a jobbing builder, in the end cottage (notice the builder's board). His uncle Albert, cab-proprietor and jobmaster, lived in the cottage on the left. The cab and fly business ended about the time of World War 1, after which Jack became a general worker. In the 1920s when the Bankside council houses were built, he dug most of the wells. This photograph is one from a collection of glass plate negatives found in Charlton.

12. Girl with a pram, outside Pond Cottage. The pram dates back to about 1890. I found this turn-of-century picture in an old stable.

13. The Post Office, before 1914. The entrance door, with board overhead, is on the left. The man outside is probably Mr. Hamlin, the postmaster. He also worked at Charlton sawmill, leaving his wife in charge of the shop. She is standing with her baby Doris and her sister Frances in the doorway at the other end, where the family lived. The eldest Hamlin daughter, also called Frances, is sitting in the middle of the seat, between her two cousins, with the summer house and wash-house behind. The notice reads, 'Teas provided and cycles stored here'; and the other notice, above the sitting room window, 'Picture postcards sold here.' You could also buy needles and cotton, elastic, and black Angora darning wool. Behind a screen in the shop there was a telephone. Mail arrived about 7.30 a.m. by horse and cart, driven by a postman with a gold-laced hat. There was a telegraph wire across the fields to the station.

14. The signpost by the pond. It points on the left to Cocking and Midhurst, and on the right to West Dean, Lavant and Chichester. A notice forbids traction engines to draw water from the pond, but they could draw it from the river opposite *The Horse and Groom.* Other parish notices are fixed below. Under the signpost was a popular place with children for playing marbles.

The thatched cottage on the left is Gerrards Garden, where Alice Groombridge lived. She took in washing; and this included the men's and boys' church surplices, which were laundered quarterly. Choirboys whose turn it was to take them to her were each paid 2d.

15. By Singleton pond, about 1905. Carts, wagons and timber drays from Charlton sawmill regularly splashed through the pond. This was to prevent the wheels from getting dry, for if this happened the wood shrank and the iron tyres worked loose. Shepherds came this way with their flocks, and drovers with cattle they had bought at Chichester market.

Alf Reeves, brother of Tom Reeves (see plate 17), lived in Apiary House (on the right). Pond Cottage (centre), said to have been sold early in the century for £50, was a part-time butcher's shop, run by Mr. Fish of Midhurst, who opened it Tuesdays, Thursdays and Saturdays. W. Miles (see plate 16), built the big wooden shed on the left. A wagonette and fly were kept here, with horses in the loose boxes between Alf's house and Tom's house Pricklows.

16. Singleton Stores, W. Miles. According to Pike's *Directory* of 1886-7, from which this bold advertisement was taken, the population of Singleton 'with the hamlet of Charlton' was then 555, and of East Dean 343.

17. Tom Reeves, carrier, lived at Pricklows, and the cart was kept in a wooden shed (now demolished) which backed up against the house. His brother Alf was often the driver, as Tom was busy with other things; he owned a timber cart, employed two men on haulage, worked in the woods, and sold bunts (small faggots). A big card with 'R' on it, placed in a front window, was the customer's signal to the carrier to call. His charge for an order was 2d to 6d. For collecting a box of 15 dozen eggs, delivering it in Chichester and returning it empty, the charge was 3d. For 6d he sometimes took a passenger to Chichester, saving him the long trek to Singleton station. To rest the horse he left it in the yard at *The Fountain* in South Street. Delivery and collection at the shops took much of the rest of his time, and it was often 9 p.m. before he was home again.

Once, when Alf was driving, the horse was startled and dazzled by car headlights, and the cart went into a bank and overturned. Not long after this accident, they changed over to a motor van. The day of the carrier's horse and cart was over. More buses and cars meant that business began to languish, and Tom turned to other things. His last job was as lengthman for the W.S.C.C. — road work, clearing drains and ditches, trimming grass verges.

18. Advertisement for Smart and Haslett, Family Grocers. Smart was formerly a builder, and a lump of builder's lead from his time is today still used as the doorstop in the village shop.

19. C. Pennicott, the village shop, and Cobbler's Row, about 1910. Pennicott's dog used to lie out in the road for mu[c]
of the day.

20. The delivery cart, about 1907. Charl[es]
Pennicott owned the shop, and his broth[er]
Fred helped him. The tarpaulin protected
the groceries from the weather. At harves[t]
and haying times there was often a 4½
gallon barrel of beer, which had been
ordered by a farmer, roped to the foot-
board, behind the horse. Pennicott was
the local agent for the supply of beer.
This cart did the deliveries as far as West
Dean and Drovers. The wagon, driven by
Bert Hoad, was used for Charlton and
East Dean. There was no milk cart; peopl[e]
fetched their own milk. Fred Pennicott
was killed in World War 1.

1. Horse-drawn dray near the bridge, returning to Charlton sawmill from the railway station, where it has just taken load of brush backs. There are two trace horses in front and one in the shafts behind. The extra one was needed for he steep pull-up to the station. The village shop has now passed to Charles Court, who has returned from the war. The inger car on the right belonged to the photographer.

22. C. Court, the village shop during the 1920s. The first petrol pumps have been installed. The store rooms above the shop were full of sacks of meal, grain, flour, slabs of butter, fruit etc. Blocks of currants and sultanas had to be brushed out and cleaned or put through a fruit-washing machine, then put in small packages — all this out of shoppi ͮ hours. Vinegar came in 12 gallon casks, syrup in 40 gallon kegs, and customers brought their own bottles, jugs or jam jars. Sometimes there were accidents, as when the tap of the syrup keg got left on; and once, after a small boy's jug had been filled with treacle, it was discovered that the money was still in the bottom.

23. Horse and Sussex wagon at Swallows Farm, Dial Post. This was low-slung and capacious but cumbersome. Note the skid pan for braking.

24. Traffic by the bridge includes a Model T Ford.

25. (*overleaf*) The village seen from the top of the church tower. Behind Little Garth (the cottage on the left) is the malthouse with its tall chimney, long since demolished. In the centre, facing the church, are two shops. The first belonged to Gus Mason, the carpenter and wheelwright, who lived at Downview. The one with the striped gable was the shoemaker's. *The Fox and Hounds* is on the right of the photograph.

26. Outside the wheelwright's shop, since demolished. Here is Gus Mason with Tom Staples, his boy apprentice. Over the shop was a storage loft.

27. (*below*) Downview with Gus Mason and his wife and daughter. The old malthouse is on the right.

28. Elizabeth and Tom Staples about 1920, soon after he came out of the army. He had been a corporal in the Army Service Corps, making wheels for wagons and gun carriages. After the war he moved his work to the black-smith's shop in Charlton Road. Here in one morning he and his apprentice Bert Dadley fitted twenty-seven iron rims to cart and wagon wheels. With the increase in motor traffic his business declined and he became the local builder, living in the house later called Staples Place.

29. (*above*) *The Fox and Hounds,* about 1905. Swings and a Try-your-strength machine are being put up for Race Week. Workers and onlookers have stopped to pose for the camera. An advertisement for *The Sportsman* is on the wall behind.

In smuggling days, women would bring the publican baskets of vegetables with brandy, tea or snuff hidden underneath. This practice was by no means confined to Singleton.

(opposite below) Outside the bakery. From left to right: Charlie Pennicott junior, the baker, who made his own ㅤast from home-grown potatoes; Phil Hoad, who swept up and was still at school; Ern Bailey, the village policeman's son, ㅤo took the pushcart to Charlton and West Dean; Leon Staples and Phil's father Bert Hoad, drivers of the horse and cart ㅤ distant rounds.

ㅤBread-making had its own routine. Tom Reeves of Pricklows supplied bunts for the oven. As soon as it was hot ㄲn as it ㅤㅤugh, the embers were swept out and the dough was put in. The baker returned at 10 p.m. to cut it back, and ㅤk, and ㅤㅤin at 4 a.m., when it needed further cutting. By 8 a.m. the loaves, some 150 or more, were ready for delivery. Buns ㅤd rolls were also made, with lard rolls a speciality. Villagers were allowed to use the bakery oven for their own cakes ㅤd pies — the charge was 1d or ½d.

ㅤThe coach party, a Women's Institute outing about 1922. Phil Norrell is the small boy looking over the door, with ㅤmother beside him. The group also includes Mrs. Pitt, Mrs. Windibank, Mrs. Phillips, Mrs. Miles, Mrs. Mabel Ansell, ㅤs. Ticehurst, Mrs. Burns, Mrs. Worthington, and Mrs. Saunders.

ㅤSingleton Church, before ㅤWellingtonia tree (left) ㅤcut down. Pen and ink ㅤwing of this 1000-year old ㅤrch by Major-General C. de ㅤㅤaussen, who lived at Prick- ㅤs in the 1960s. The Church, ㅤover a century mistakenly ㅤㅤed St. John's, in 1979 was ㅤㅤedicated under its original ㅤㅤe of St. Mary's.

Singleton Church.

33.   Ladies' cricket in 1747 — 'the Maids of Charlton and Singleton' against those of West Dean and Chilgrove, all 'decked in blue coloured ribbons.' It was played on the Artillery Ground, London, and 'when the Company broke in' turned out to be a very rough game indeed, 'some being very much frightened and others hurt.' Play had to be suspended till the next day. There is no record as to which side won.

Note the long curved bat, the two short stumps with single bail, and the underarm bowling.

34.   The return match in 1947, won by Singleton. Here is Beatrice Kerridge, top scorer with 29, being chaired by her team, which includes Eileen Mitchell, Peggy Pettingale, Enid Davies, Doris Knight, Joyce Ticehurst, Peggy Howard, Olive Brown, Mrs. Miller and Nora Laishley.

5. (*right*) Singleton school in winter snow. Built in 1852, the school was given to the village by the Rector, the Rev. F. A. Bowles. The porch was added in 1894. Behind the school is St. Francis Cottage, dating from between 1350 and 1400 and probably the oldest in Singleton. Originally it had a central hall about 18 feet square, with an opening in the roof where the chimney now is.

At the turn of the century Arthur Smith, a carter from Cucumber Farm, lived here. He was also the local barber for men and boys. His clients came in the evening, always two at a time, one to have his hair cut (price twopence) while the other held the candle.

274

June 28th Flogged John Gray for open defiance of authority & impudence. Acquainted the Rector of same punishment.
This boy at Recreation time went home & did not return
His mother, Mrs Gray came to School— struck & abused me, refusing to send him to School

36. (*left*) Mr. Percy Windo, headmaster from 1898-1901 (salary £140 p. a., with house), had problems with the Gray family, as this entry of his in the school log book shows. He was a harsh disciplinarian and caned for insolence, negligence, persistent talking, laziness, 'disobedience and moral faults,' and also 'cruelty to a bee'.

7. (*right*) Mr. Kibblewhite and his boys, 1904-5. Mr. Kibblewhite took over the school in 1901 and his wife was in charge of the infants. Jeff Farley (second row, fourth from the left) has said: 'We wore white celluloid collars — easy to wash, knickerbockers fastened below the knee, long black stockings with elastic garters, and hobnailed boots with toe and heel pieces. Mr. Kibblewhite was kind but stood no nonsense, and when he used the cane he used it. We respected and obeyed him.' He put about sixty good books into the Reading Room, sang in the church choir, got up a Mummers' play and arranged concerts. He was prime mover of the harvest supper at Manor Farm and also organised local festivities for Edward VII's coronation.

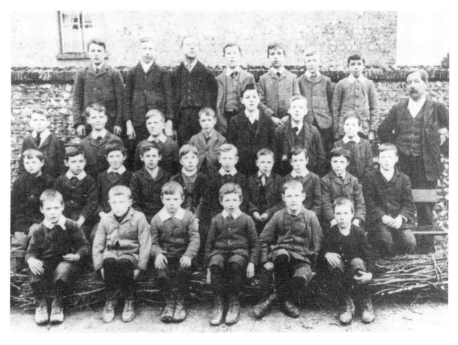

38. (*above*) Charlton Road, Singleton, about 1903, as it was shortly before Dr. Garratt came. He bought the flint stables (le of the two children, Eddie Bartlett and his young sister) and th house (far left with white door) from the Duke of Richmond. turned the stables into a surgery, waiting room and dispensary, with a sitting room above. He put the first telephone in Singlet in the surgery, sharing a party line with West Dean Park. Patien came on Wednesday and Saturday afternoons.

The house on the right is Kingsham Cottage. The four stabl (centre) were mainly used for Goodwood Race Week. They we demolished in the 1920s. Behind the stables was a path leading a sweetshop.

39. Dr. G. C. Garratt, O.B.E., M.D., a scholar and gold medall of St. Bartholemew's Hospital, with a Cambridge degree in Nat Sciences, came to the Chichester district in 1905. In addition t his wide country practice he had his main surgery in Chichestei and also became the first visiting physician at Aldingbourne Sanatorium and later at Graylingwell Hospital. In 1910 he bec a consultant to the Royal West Sussex Hospital.

He is still widely remembered as a kind, knowledgeable and devoted doctor. He did his own dispensing and made his visits foot, by bicycle or car. One message found in his letterbox reac 'Come at once. Dying,' with name and address given. He cycled off to a remote hamlet, only to find that the 'dying' patient had recovered and gone for a walk. Another message was: 'Bab refuses to take nourishment — got convulsions'. On arrival Dr. Garratt quickly made his diagnosis: 'Rage and frustration. The teat of the bottle hasn't been pierced.' From the downstairs ro of a West Dean cottage he was once heard to open the front do march upstairs, into a bedroom and out again, downstairs, the out as he shut the door behind him, 'Wrong house!'

After his retirement Dr. Garratt spent his final years in his Singleton house. When he died on 8 February 1940, there was hearse. Tom Staples and his men carried the coffin to the ceme by the River Lavant. On his tombstone are engraved the words 'Beloved physician.'

40. (*right*) Nurse Harding, M.B.E., district nurse from 1910 to 1957, was a tower of strength, especially in the days when Dr. Garratt had no partner. 'If Nurse Harding says it's all right, it's all right,' he used to say, relieved that he could entrust much responsible work to her. Calm, determined, shrewd in judgment, a tireless round-the-clock worker, she was a remarkable woman. As one of her patients said, 'Wherever she was needed, she was there.'

41. A visit from the district nurse, at Charlton Farmhouse. Nurse Harding was one of the first district nurses to be given a car — an open Austin 7, with a very short clutch which she never entirely mastered. It leapt into the air when she started up, and boys loved to watch her 'taking off.'

42. (*above*) Charlie Treagus outside Dr.
Garratt's house. He lived in a rent-free flint
house in Bankside when he looked after the
horses at Manor Farm. In 1901, after receiving
his £3 bonus for harvest work, he walked
with his wife to Chichester, his small daughter
on his shoulders — up Town Lane to the
Trundle, down the chalk road, all seven miles.
He spent his £3 on a coat and trousers for
himself and winter clothes for his wife and
child. Then they walked home over the downs
with their parcels.

   Dr. Garratt's house was usually let during
Goodwood Race Week. Jeff Farley (see plate
37) remembered how as a small boy, when
the actress Lillie Langtry was once the tenant,
he looked over the garden wall and saw her
having tea on the lawn with King Edward VII.
The royal visitor used to stable his race horses
at Childown, near the bridge.

43. Margery, her older sister Cornelia and
Bert Reed, 1917. The photographer's side-car
is in the background. When Margery was fifteen,
she went to the doctor's house to work for Mrs.
Garratt.

Littlewood Farm, about 1902. The cattle are short-horns, and the long low mound in front of the flint wall is a [cl]amp, probably with mangolds for cattle-feed. To the right of the clamp is a pile of flints picked up from the fields [an]d ready to be steam-rolled into the road. A modern photo shows that the white gate, the low wall, the pig-sties [an]d most of the trees have now gone, and the road is metalled and much wider. It used to be the old coach road, which [th]e poet John Keats took when he came to Chichester on a mild January day in 1819.

(*opposite above*) The old coach road, after passing through [Sing]leton, winds up the hill to the Trundle. This part is known [loca]lly as Town Lane and in the 1960s it was widened. Carriages from [Sing]leton station to Goodwood races came this way, and in Race Week [the] horses were kept at the bottom of the hill to help if carriages got [stuc]k on the way up.

(*opposite below*) Here, in this modern photograph, it continues [nor]th over the shoulder of the Trundle. It must have been quite as [rou]gh, rutted and pot-holed when the London coach came this way. [Sus]sex roads were notoriously about the worst in the country, and [ther]e were many jokes about them. I wrote a verse based on one:

> 'Do I see a hat in the road?' I said.
> I picked up the hat — and I saw a head.
> I pulled out a man, who said, 'Don't go.
> Help pull out my horse. He's down below.'

[In t]his picture the felled beeches are being loaded for Shoreham [Harb]our, for shipment to Sweden to be made into paper.

(*above*) Wounded soldiers from Graylingwell Military Hospital [bein]g entertained by members of the Women's Institute, in 1916. Once [a m]onth they gave a tea party for them and a social evening at the [scho]ol. They also knitted comforts for the Merchant Navy, made shirts [for s]oldiers and bandages for hospitals, and helped farmers by growing [vege]tables on Lamb Down. It was largely out of the desire to help a [nati]on already at war that Singleton W.I., the first in England, was [foun]ded.

(*right*) Bob Farley, who was killed on the Somme in 1916.

Kriegsgefangenensendung.

Absender:

Baracke Nr. _H. B. 5_

Kdo.: _Lazaret_

Munsterlager (Prov. Hannover)

Deutschland.

My Dear Dad I am wounded in right forearm, prisoner address on other side, send parcels quickly, money if possible, I am in no pain so do not worry, they treat us very well, send parcel every week four cards two letters a month cheer up do not worry love to all Auntie Jeff

49. (*above*) Jeff Farley Bob's brother, wounded P.O.W. He was taken prisoner in the same battle and sent this post-card home from his P.O.W. camp in Germany. The wound in his arm prevented him from writing any more than the beginning 'My Dear Dad' and the ending; the rest was written by a friend.

50. (*opposite above*) Jeff Farley in dark cap, seated far left, and other prisoners outside the Lazaret (sick bay) of the Munsterlager in the snow. They were English, Australian, Russian, Belgian, French — all nationalities — and the winter was bitterly cold. Jeff helped one of them to escape, but he was soon recaptured.

The thought of his Singleton home must have helped to keep him going. His father was a builder, carpenter and undertaker, who made wooden churns as well as coffins (£2 for an adult's coffin, 10s for a child's). Jeff was the last of a direct line dating back in church registers to 1650, when the family first came to the village. At the end of the war he returned on a hospital ship carrying exchanged P.O.W.'s. As the train came out of Drove Tunnel, chugged past Cucumber Farm and gave him his first sight of Singleton, he felt he was home for good.

Jeff, who died in 1979 aged 81, was a humorous character and a do-it-yourself philosopher. 'Things will be worse you know' he cheerfully predicted. 'That's a good way of looking at it. If they get better you're pleased; if they get worse you're prepared.'

51. (*above*) Dedication of the War Memorial, outside the church, 1919.

52. (*above*) Maypole dance on the village green, part of the Peace Celebrations, 1919.

53. Britannia's wagon, in the procession to the Leys meadow, pauses outside the surgery. Lady Maxwell of Grove House is Britannia, the small boy beside her in a sailor cap Ted Court, the tall boy-scout (left) Charlie Tizzard, and the white smocked figure (right) Charlie Treagus.

Charlton

Northward, and rising close above the town,
Another mountain's known by Levin(g) Down;
a Piranean path is still there seen,
where Devon's Duke, full speed, did drive his well
bred courser down, and flying, leap't five bars;
incredible the act! but still 'twas fact.

from the anonymous poem of 1737. The Duke of Devonshire, like the Duke of St. Alban's and other aristocrats, owned a cottage at Charlton in the days of the great Charlton Hunt

54. Charlton, Levin Down (left) and Charlton Forest, the scene of what was once the premier hunt in England, photographed from the air. Half the aristocracy and distinguished visitors from Europe too came here during the hunting season. The Duke of Devonshire and the Duke of St. Albans had houses in Charlton, and the neighbouring villages were full of aristocratic visitors. The clump of beeches on top of Levin Down was planted for the Duke of Richmond by French prisoners during the Napoleonic wars.

(*right*) Charles, 2nd Duke of Richmond, painted when
[Ear]l of March, in a white coat ornamented with gold. He was
[Du]ke when the Charlton Hunt was at the height of its fame.
[In 1]730 Fox Hall was built for him as a hunting lodge.

[5]7 & 58.   The famous Charlton Hunt.

'and horses too, the best of blood were bought,. . .
of middle size, with nostrils wide and red.'

[...] Carey (above), son of Grey Ramsden, hunter, 1738-1740.
[A gro]om in red undress livery is carrying his saddle.
[Re]d Robin, bay hunter, 1742. A groom in livery holds the
[...] and a hunting whip. Saddle and cloth are on the ground,
[t]he cathedral and harbour are in the distance.
[Ti]pster, hound, 1733, son of Lord Ta . . . .l's Monster and
[D]uke of Richmond's Friskey.

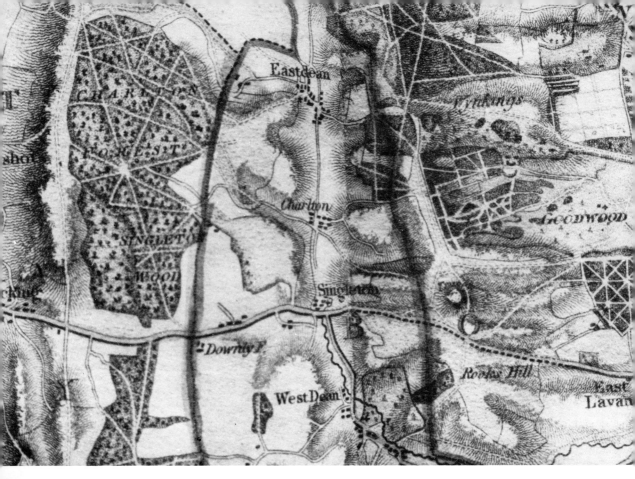

59. (*opposite above*) The Rape of Chichester, 1815, from Dallaway's *Western Sussex*, 1815.

> 'In this sweet vale, by hill and downs enclosed,
> an age ago, Diana fixed her court.'

Diana was the Roman goddess of hunting. The quotations are from the long anonymous poem of 1737.

60. (*opposite below*) Tom Johnson's cottage. The most famous of all Charlton huntsmen, he was huntsman during 'the greatest chase that ever was', the run of Friday 26 January 1738, in which a fox was hunted for 10 hours and more than 57 miles. It was a contest to decide which was the best hunt, and the 'Gentlemen of Charlton' won. When Tom Johnson died on 20 December 1774, the Second Duke of Richmond placed a memorial tablet to his memory in Singleton Church:

> 'Here Johnson lies. What Hunter can deny
> Old, honest Tom the Tribute of a Sigh?
> Deaf is that Ear, which caught the opening Sound;
> Dumb is that Tongue, which cheered the Hills around.
> Unpleasing Truth — Death hunts us from our Birth
> In view; and Men, like Foxes, take to Earth.'

61. (*below*) A meet at the Kennels, Goodwood. Designed by Wyatt, this is perhaps his best building at Goodwood. It is now the Golf-Club house.

62 & 63. Nos. 30 and 31 Charlton. The second photograph is an enlargement of the figure in the white dress on the right.

64. (*opposite above*) This photograph shows the sawmill from Fox Hall. While the Fosters lived there, the allotments in the foreground and the orchard behind belonged to them. The building at the back is a tall one, as the shafting and belting drive were overhead.

65. (*opposite below*) Charlton sawmill before World War 1, when Thomas Foster ran it. The tall building on the left is the main mill, where the sawing was done. It contained one large band-saw, two rack benches (circular saw and moving table, automatic) and six or seven push benches, on which the timber was pushed through by hand. It was lit from skylights, and after dark from paraffin lamps hanging from the roof. The dark building on the right is a timber store, and the low building (far right) part of the brush-back drying shed. The fenced field was used for grazing horses. These photographs are both from glass plate negatives.

66. The boy with the penny-farthing. This is Thomas Foster's son Harold, who worked at the sawmill and di in early manhood after an accident there. In those days there were no extractor pipes to carry the sawdust awa to the boiler fires, and it was left about the site in big p Harold was filling a sack when the pile slipped, knocke him down and covered him. Badly hurt internally, he a month later.

Penny-farthings were very popular between 1870 an 1890. They cost from £8 to £20 each and were not as hard to ride as they looked, but you had to look out f pot-holes. A plunger brake was sometimes fitted, but i was tricky to use. The best way to slow down was by pressing back on the pedals.

67. (*left*) Fox Hall, a modern photograph. Designed b Lord Burlington, it has three storeys, finely detailed window surrounds, and a tall first floor room with gild ceiling.

68 & 69. (*opposite*) Meadow Cottage. The manager o the sawmill used to live here. In 1886-7 this was Alfre Parslow, and the three ladies were probably in his hou hold.

70. (*above*) *The Fox*, formerly *The Pig and Whistle*, an L-shaped 18th-century flint building, with red brick dressings and quoins. It is heavily beamed and has wide fireplaces and brick floors. This inn was the meeting place of the first Women's Institute in England.

71. (*left*) A game of Solo Whist at *The Fox*. Phil Laishley (publican), Frank Miles, James Read, Mr. Jones (from Bognor), and Horrie Austin.

72. (*above right*) Edmund Harvey, licensee in 1886-7.

73. (*far right*) John Kennett, licensee of *The Fox* in 1890, with his wife and family — Lily, Victoria, Charle Egbert, Walter and Leonard. Mother and father were so busy upstairs getting themselves and the younger children ready for the photographer that they forgot to mak Walter change his muddy breeches. Egbert went to Australia, and Walter became a carter at Croydon. His life ended tragically when the horses in his brewer's dra bolted and he was trampled trying to stop them.

74. Young postman, probably at Fox Hall. Like others of the Charlton collection, this photograph is from a glass plate negative.

5. (*above*) Horse and cart postal delivery at Charlton, early
in the century.

6. Mr. Dyer, the postman, outside his Charlton cottage,
with his wife and daughter, about 1923. After sorting the
mail at Singleton Post Office, he usually did the delivery
on foot. He had a springy step and used to lope from
house to house.

77.   Road-making in the 1920s. A pile of stones is ready for the steam-roller to roll in.

78.   (*opposite above*) Farm group, Charlton. The labour force on a single farm, about 1890. The whiskered figure (second from the left) is probably Jesse Phillips, the rick builder — he's holding a thatching truss used for carrying straw up to the roof. Next to him is the shepherd, with a crook in his left hand and a Welsh collie sheepdog at his feet. The tall man behind him is holding a wooden barn scoop. It was large and light and used for shovelling grain or chaff. In the middle is the boot boy. Next but one to him a man is holding a long serrated knife. This was dragged behind two horses to cut the grass; the teeth were riveted on. Here it has been taken off to be laid on a carpenter's trestle and sharpened with a flat file. On the extreme right stands the cowman, with his white apron and burnished milk pails, which had to be kept clean and stainless. Behind him the bowler-hatted man with the faghook is Billy Wells. He worked on the farm for most of the year, but during the winter he made sheep hurdles in the wood. As an old man he was almost bent double with rheumatism — a not uncommon fate in those days for men who had worked in the woods for most of their lives. The group also includes a Croucher and a Miles, who drove the binder. The barn at the back has long been demolished.

79.   Moses Osborne outside no. 27 Charlton, about 1922, with Molly Gable and her daughter, who both lived here. Moses lived at no. 43. A woodman on the Goodwood Estate, he kept the copses in good shape, trimmed up the rides and cleared them for the winter shooting. In his later years he did general forestry work nearer home. His son Harry also worked in the woods.

80. (*above*) Teddy Wadey, who worked at the sawmill, leading horses into the forest to collect timber. They are in tandem, so as to avoid the wheel ruts. Previously he had worked for Tom Reeves, the carrier and haulier.

81. (*above right*) Unknown lady, smartly dressed for the photographer, with garden table and flowers.

82. (*right*) Charlton Farmhouse, red brick, built in the 18th century, is described in the 1737 poem:

> ' . . . . and here a regular front, full south appears
> a Double Palace which two friends did rear;
> the strong Cavendo owns the part of one,
> Farquier his friend in attic storey sleeps.
> Furious Harcourt did the other build,
> and great was the expense and charge of both.'

83. Carriages for Race Week at Goodwood leaving Chichester Station and the Globe Hotel, about 1900.

Goodwood

84. (*above*) The grandstand was built by the fifth Duke of Richmond. It was 120 feet long and is said to have held 3,000 people. On the ground floor were refreshment and retiring rooms, on the first floor betting rooms and a glass-fronted saloon, and on top a steeply raked open terrace with benches and railings. This splendid setting for Goodwood in its heyday attracted kings, queens, dukes, duchesses, and great numbers of aristocrats to some of the best racing in the country. They travelled here by carriage over some of the roughest roads in the kingdom, then put up locally in the surrounding villages.

85. Goodwood Races, 31 July 1875, view from down the course. Notice the open course, the fairground booths, the beech trees which so delighted Queen Alexandra.

86. (*left*) The finish, a close one, as seen from the Trundle, with race-goers swarming on to the course as soon as the horses have passed.

37. The crowd in 1875. Outside the grandstand and enclosure, the crowd was pretty rough and the atmosphere more like that of a fairground than an aristocratic racecourse. Notice the roundabouts and coconut shies, the ragged children with bottles.

38. Winner's horse-shoe. During Race Week many of the runners were stabled in Singleton. The stables adjoining Dr. Garratt's house were built specially for them, and a shoe from each winner was afterwards nailed to the door of the stable it had occupied. Perhaps Miss Toto was the winner of the race depicted in plate 36.

89 & 90.   Race Week at the turn of th
century. The aristocratic grandstand ha
not yet made way for the Edwardian o
The course is fully open, and the road
Chichester little more than a chalky tr
In the second photograph (*left*) carriag
have gathered, facing in the direction c
Singleton station, ready to take racego
away.

91.   (*below left*) The Edwardian granc
stand. Goodwood was still a great soci
occasion, though the quality of the ra
was not up to the Ascot standard. In 1
the seventh Duke of Richmond, to att
new customers, pulled down the 1830
stand (which had cost £346) and built
new one (£37,000). It was four times
long as the old stand and stretched fro
the lawn to the boundary of the paddc
There was a Press stand at the west en
and a subway under the whole of the f
By using the subway the ladies could r
the paddock without having to battle t
way through the crowd outside. The r
pavilion can be seen on the extreme rig
Nairn and Pevsner describe the stand a
'a jolly Edwardian building, like an enl
Oxford College barge.'
    The work involved caused so much
damage to the road at the back that it
to be remade. For this local horses and
carts brought up 125 tons of flints fro
East Dean Farm, a gang of navvies wa
engaged, and three steamrollers hired.

92 & 93.   (*opposite above and below*)
King Edward VII and Queen Alexandr
the royal pavilion. From the front the
pavilion looks simple enough, though
it was luxuriously furnished. The King
private lavatory was in marble, with r
monogram, mahogany seat and silver-
flushing handle. In the view below, nc
the judges' box on the left.

94. (*above*) The race-cours from the Trundle, which wa open to the public. There w no admission charges here. horses on the right have jus finished their race, using th lower slopes to slow down. 1909 the Duke of Portland' horse Roche Abbey won th Singleton Plate — but could stop. Unseating the jockey, galloped up the Trundle, disappeared over the top, a was last seen heading for th Hampshire border.

95. (*left*) Fashionable dres on the course, outside the Edwardian grandstand.

96. (*below left*) The Pheas at Goodwood.

East Dean

As I came along between Upwaltham and Eastdean, ...
I saw, with great delight, a pig at almost every labourer's
house. The houses are good and warm; and the gardens
some of the very best that I have seen in England . . . .
The lane goes along through some of the finest farms
in the world.

from *Rural Rides* by William Cobbett (1762-1835)

97. (*above*) Droke Lane, between Upwaltham and East Dean. This is the way that William Cobbett (1763-1835) came on horse-back one wet August day in 1823. He was soaked to the skin and suffering from what he called 'the hooping cough.' Near here a young turnip-hoer, sheltering under the hedge and breakfasting on a lump of bread and bacon, told him where he could find a good inn. Then on he rode through East Dean to Singleton. Here he had breakfast at the inn (probably *The Fox and Hounds*) and in front of a fire 'dried my shirt on my back. We shall see what this does for a hooping cough.' The remedy worked; it cured him of a cough which had been troubling him since March.

98.   Hay cart in Droke Lane, before 1905. This Scotch cart or long cart could turn in its own length and was handy for hills.

99. (*above*) Old cottage, about 1922. With its mullioned windows under the half-hipped gables, this is architecturally perhaps the most interesting cottage in the village.

100. An old lady in the porch.

91. (*above*) Road-mending outside *The
Star and Garter* Inn, about 1913. The
stones were picked up on the fields by
piece-workers, sold to the W.S.C.C.,
carted by the farmer to the road-side,
then left to be rolled in by the steam-
roller. A grocery delivery cart stands
outside the inn. Notice the two posts
and cross-piece (right foreground), which
mark a spring bubbling up in the road.
The Rev. W. J. H. Newman M.A., the
vicar, used to call this 'the pub-loafer's
perch'. On the left is the Post Office,
opened in 1891. Mrs. Sarah White was
postmistress for thirty years.

92. *The Star and Garter* Inn, the
advertisement in Pike's *Directory* for
1886-7.

93. (*bottom right*) White smocks were
often Sunday wear in earlier days. On the
left is Harold Kewell, landlord of *The Star
and Garter*.

**The Star and Garter Inn,
EAST DEAN.**

JAMES STEER, Proprietor.

*Situated in a beautiful hollow of the Downs, near Goodwood, 3 miles
from Singleton Station.*

PURE WINES AND SPIRITS.   EXCELLENT STABLING.

Accommodation for Beanfeasts or Pleasure Parties.   Parties can be met by arrangement.

104.   Cleaning out the pond, a 'goodwill job' done by volunteers in 1905. Dung carts were very robust and could each carry a ton of flints. At hay-time and harvest they were fitted with ladders and helped to carry hay and sheaves.

105.   The pond, about 1920. The water-cart, with pump, hose and spray, was used for filling the troughs in the fields, also for spraying roads during road-making. *The Star and Garter* is behind, and (right) the sheds where Mr. Whitney, who mended chair legs, and Mr. Hopkins worked.

106. A ball game in Butcher's End cottages, about 1904. The three figures on the left are Mrs. Reeves, Mrs. Osborne and her daughter Kitty (with the ball). The Rev. W. J. H. Newman is on the far right. Two outside wells served the whole block. The families living here, one to each cottage, were Goodwood tenants. By the terms of letting, no business and no lodgers were allowed, and a week's notice on either side could terminate a tenancy. The landlord attended to outside repairs. The tenants had 'to keep cottages clean and tidy, the chimneys regularly swept, the windows mended, and the inside walls whitewashed' (lime supplied by the landlord). No dung or ashes were allowed near the cottages.

107. (*overleaf*) In the garden behind Butcher's End cottages. Left to right: Jack Hall, Mrs. West, Mr. West, Mrs. Osborne with (in front) her sons Ernie and Reg, Kathleen (Kitty) Osborne.

108. The vicar with children by the pond, about 1908. The signpost points to (left) Goodwood, Chichester, (right) Upwaltham, Petworth. Yew Cottage and Court Hill are behind.

109. Motor-bike and chair, in 1905, on the day the pond was cleaned out. In the back on the left are the men who did the job — Thomas Smith, his brother George, and Frank Lillywhite. Tommy Johnson is sitting on the motor-bike, with 70 year old Charles Oakley (who sang in the church choir) in front. The owner of the motor-bike, the East Dean shopkeeper, invited them to sit there for the photograph. On the right is Jack Poling, the blacksmith, with his son Ted on the pony. Ted served in the navy in World War I and died of pneumonia soon after. Notice the fine corn rick in the background.

110.   Remember, remember,
The fifth of November,
And the bonfire that blazed too soon.

In 1905 there was a corn rick (see plate 109) dangerously close to the usual village green site for the annual bonfire, so it was decided to celebrate more safely on the top of Court Hill. Here is a party of boys helping to take up the wood and stack the bonfire. Some practical joker crowned it with an effigy, not of Guy Fawkes, but of Mr. Lambert the keeper; then, unable to wait till the proper date, he put a match to it.

111.   The blacksmith's shop, 1905. Jack Poling, the blacksmith, is on the left, with his son Ted on the horse. His assistant Ernest Oakley has his hand on the open door. The girl on the right is Jack's daughter Ivy. Notice the wagon wheel, the watering can and setting out table in front. On bonding day the red-hot iron tyre was hammered into position round the wheel, then splashed with a can of water from the pond, so that the iron contracted. What with the smoke, the hissing steam, and the acrid smell of burning wood, this was a moment that children especially loved to watch. The notice on the left reads, 'Vote for Talbot' (Lord Edward Talbot, conservative).

112. East Dean Church, about 1900.

113. Church choir stalls and font before 1905.

114. The wedding of Ernest West and Amy Norrell in 1905. The vicar disliked charging his parishioners for a wedding. When Ernest gave him the 7/6 fee, he made a present of it to the bride.

15.   The village band at the turn of the century. Their instruments included cornets, trombones, cymbals and bass
rum. They used to practise in an old stable by the vicarage and were in great demand for fêtes and festivals. On May
ay they played by the pond, where a Maypole was put up for the dancers. These were mostly girls, but a few boys —
uch teased by others not included — were also chosen. Once a year there was a special concert to raise money for the
ospital. Mrs. Amy West was always there to help with refreshments, and Farmer Stratton collected the money —
ually about £10 — and kept order.

  After World War 1 was over, the band played on the green every Sunday morning. They played until the chapel
lk had gone into their service and the door closed behind them. Then, still playing, they marched up to the church,
th the congregation trooping along behind them, to attend the service.

ont row: Charlie Phillips, Harry Gumbleton (bandmaster), Walt Reed, Charlie Waymark.

ick row: James Croucher, William Gumbleton, Charlie Johnson, Albert Ede, Arch Rudwick, Gilbert Switzer,
eorge Waymark.

HENRY HOPKINS,

𝔅uilder, ℭontractor, and 𝔘ndertaker,

HILL COTTAGE, EAST DEAN.

116. Henry Hopkins, builder.

117. Henry Hopkins being visited by the vicar in his cottage on Court Hill. Remembered as 'Grandpy', he was an excellent carpenter and a churchwarden for many years.

118. (*below*) The vicarage in the Rev. W. J. H. Newman's time. Today, when one priest looks after three parishes, it is a private house.

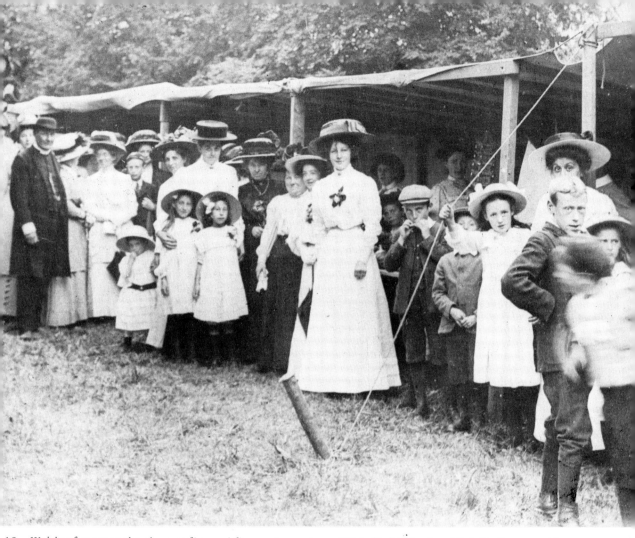

19.   Waiting for tea at the vicarage fête and flower show, about 1912. (Left) the Rev. W. J. H. Newman; Mrs. Amy West, with her two small girls in front of her; (centre) Kate Osborne, in white dress. Everyone seems more interested n the camera than in the tune Jack Johnson is playing on the mouth-organ.

20.   *(overleaf above)* The Church Army mission van, 1901 or 1902. It went from parish to parish in spring or early ummer, staying about two weeks, after which a local farmer supplied a horse to tow it on to another village. The icar is with Alice Poling on the left. The two young parsons lived, ate and slept in the van, and one of them would reach in church on Sunday. The meetings for the children were held by the van. The boy with the cricket bat is eonard Norrell, who was killed in World War I.

21.   *(overleaf below)* The Chapel mission van, about 1911. The Benthall brothers, non-conformists from Worthing, ere in charge, and there was keen rivalry with the Church mission.

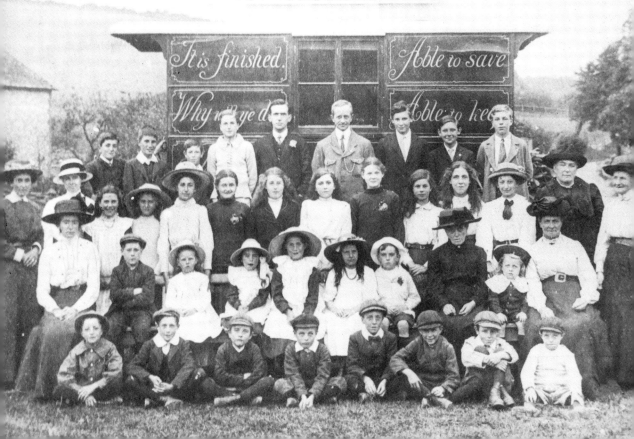

22. (*above*) East Dean Cricket Club, 1885. Front row: ? , Harry or Jerry Austin, Henry West, Wild, William Reeves. Middle row: Chitty, West (father of Henry), Austin, Waymark, ? . Back row: 1. Leggatt, 7. Henry Hopkins.

23. (*opposite above*) East Dean children

24. (*opposite below*) Children outside the village school, about 1914. Arch Long (centre, with white collar) joined the Army at 16, having added a year to his age, and served for 4½ years. Afterwards he worked for the Goodwood Estate, for a Midhurst timber merchant, and later as a warrener for the Forestry Commission, catching rabbits.

(Front row) Doris Brown, Bessie West, Dennis Reed, Jim Long, Basil Kennett, Ruby White, Donald Croucher, Bob and Addy Croucher.

(Middle row) Charlie Kennett, Percy Thompson, Clem Croucher, Arch Long, Rhys Reed, Tom Moss, P. Moss.

(Back row) Phil Wild, Jack Phillips, Vic Lambert, Fred Stevens, Fred Gorringe.

25. (*above*) The sheep-wash at Lavant

26. (*right*) Shepherd Smith, wearing his smock, about 1865.
This must be the oldest photograph in the collection. Shepherds'
smocks were worn for work well into this century, and they had
special ones for church on Sunday. They were important people
and well paid. In 1860 Shepherd Ford, Mrs. White's father, who
worked at Colworth Farm, West Dean, earned 15 shillings a week,
which remained the wage for many years. Sometimes he got a £2
bonus for the seven week lambing season. He could also have all
the rabbits he could catch.

127. (*left*) Bill Taylor, West Dean shepherd, with his dog, at Home Farm. 'I was strict with my dogs, but never knock them about. A good sheep dog has no use for anyone but i master.' Bill Taylor worked for 41 years with Mr. Cox at Preston Farm. His pay was five shillings a week when he started, 41 shillings when he married, and £13.10s in 1965 when he retired. 'I had to be vet as well as shepherd. If a ev had foot-rot, I cut it out myself.'

128. (*below*) Charlie Waymark, East Dean shepherd, at th dew pond at Postles on the way to Heyshott, about 1921. He worked for Charles Pitt of New House Farm. The sheep are Southdowns and the two dogs Old English.

129. (*opposite above*) Henry Wild, hurdle-maker, at work 1902, with the vicar and (probably) his brother Arthur Newman. When downland sheep-farming was at its height, there was a huge demand for hurdles. At one time there were seven men at East Dean making them. Henry once ma one in 22 minutes, a local record; the average worker woul make about twelve in a day. The weekly wage was fifteen shillings, but by 1920 it was £3. The underwood took 8 to 12 years to grow, depending on the ground.

0. (*above*) Horrie Austin, Ernie Austin's brother, making
rdles in 1950. He once managed to make 16 in a day. Even
ter losing the use of his right arm in World War 1, he could
ll manage 8.

1. (*right*) Ernie Austin, hurdle-maker and bee-keeper, in
71. He took over the bees from his father and continued to
ake honey, winning many awards for it, including silver cups.

132. (*above*) Spar-making at The Stables, before 1904. On the left Tom Kennett is making thatching spars; behind him Robert Kennett, carter, is making hurdles. On the right Henry West is cleaving thatching spars.

133. (*right*) 'Somebody's Dinner'. W. Kennett, rabbit-catcher, in 1908. Employed by the Goodwood Estate, he was paid fifteen shillings a week on day work, or 6d a rabbit on piece work. Alf Reeves the carrier charged him 2d to collect his catch and take it to Chichester to be sold. A rabbit was sold by weight, and the skin was worth 2d or 3d to the butcher.

134. (*left*) A two-speed ploughing engine at work. Engines such as this, with a powerful winch and a cable fitted under the boiler, were built by John Fowler & Co. of Leeds as early as 1870. They usually stood in pairs, one at each end of the field, while the plough (seen here on the right) churned its way from end to end, each engine working in turn. In the 1920s a pair was used above Bottom Barn on Charlton Down. As the drivers were out of sight of each other, they would signal by whistle when it was time for the change-over of engines. One was also used on the steepest part of Town Lane when a road-making steamroller got stuck and had to be hauled up.

5. (above) A threshing outfit arrives at
...rlings Farm, about 1910. It belonged to
...red Gadd of Heyshott and he hired it out.
...consisted of a 1907 Burrell single crank
...ction engine, a threshing machine (known
...ally as a 'drum'), a living van, elevator and
...ver huller. Coal was supplied by the farmer
...d had to be enough to get the outfit on to
...e next farm. The driver, steersman and
...sistant were not well paid and had to find
...ir own food. They slept in the living van,
...ich only had one small window — high up
...the far side — and there was often a fight
...get the top bunk. The cost of the outfit
...s about £1,300.

...& 137. (right) Record crop of Dalmeny
...s at Goodwood, August 1916. To make
...m for the horses, the first swath, round
...outside of the field, was usually cut by
...d. As more and more men went off to
...War, the self-binders were used for the
...le job.

...8. (overleaf) Threshing machine at work
...tein Farm, before 1914. Charles Pitt, the
...ver (on the left) with his white dog, was
...en the machine by George Atkins of
...nor Farm, for whom he used to work. He
...ed it out. Also in the picture are Doug
...ith (centre, with beard), George Waymark
...l man behind him), Jack Oakley (who
...the drum), Stevens (who cut the bands).
...the right of the cart are Gilbert Switzer
...l Tom Reed (who did the sacking).

139. (*above*) Moses West and his so
Richard outside the vicarage, 1904.
Moses was a carter on Manor Farm.

140. Henry West, with one of the
horses he looked after, about 1907.
His wife, in a white dress, is behind
the fence. In 1907 there were more
than a million working horses in the
country. Many farm horses went of
to World War 1. By 1967 there wer
only 2,000 working horses left.

141. The last cart. Carts and wagons, made by village craftsmen and proudly passed on from father to son, were in their final days sometimes left by the roadside to rot.

142. 'The workmen's tribute' at the funeral of the Duke of Richmond, grandfather of the present Duke.

143. West Dean Park, from an engraving in James Dallaway's 'Western Sussex', 1815. Built in 1804 by James Wyatt for the first Lord Selsey, it is described by Ian Nairn and Nikolaus Pevsner in *Buildings of England* as 'a limp Gothick house, all flint . . . Only the north part remains as Wyatt left it.'

West Dean

He wanted an easy life, and that everybody should be friends.

Wilfred Scawen Blunt (1840-1922) about Edward VII

144. West Dean Park, as it looked after George & Peto's alterations in 1893. They have added a porch wide enough to admit carriages, and on top of it a tower 'in Arts-and-Crafts Gothic.' William James, a rich American whose money came from railways and copper mines in the U.S.A., had bought the house and 11,000 acre estate and now lived here.

145. The front hall, with African hunting trophies. Arthur and Frank James, Willie's brothers, were prominent in opening up Africa from Somalia to the south for big game hunting. Frank was killed by an elephant.

46. Some of the guests for Goodwood Week, July 1895. Mrs. James is on the left.

47. House party, July 1894. Willie James is in the back row, third from the left. His wife Evelyn, who quickly
ecame a well known society hostess, is sitting on a stool, centre. The others are some of the aristocratic guests who
ave been invited to stay during Goodwood Week.

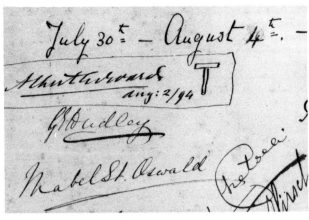

148, 149 & 150. Some signatures in the Visitors' Book.
These include Albert Edward, Prince of Wales (later Edw
VII); his wife Princess (later Queen) Alexandra; their un
married daughter Princess Victoria; their daughter Maud
and Prince Charles of Denmark, whom she married in
1896; Prince George (later George V) and his wife Princ
(later Queen) Mary. Lady St. Oswald, a frequent guest,
took a prominent part in the amateur theatricals.

151. Amateur theatricals, 9 January 1894. The printed
programme for the two plays, 'Sweethearts' and 'Tears'
with a watercolour sketch signed by the players, in the
Visitors' Book. Evelyn James was a talented amateur ac

A royal house party for Goodwood, 24 July 1899. As Prince of Wales, and r as King, Edward VII loved country se parties, and West Dean Park was a urite choice for Goodwood Week. It a great honour to be allowed to be osts. Willie James (on the ground, t, in this picture) met him at Singleton on, while Mrs. James (here seen on the ce's left) welcomed him at the front ance of the house. Room had also to be d for private secretaries and a large of servants. Any other guests had to e royal approval. Before dinner, the meal of the day, they lined up outside door till Edward appeared with Mrs. es on his arm, then went in and sat n to the ten or twelve courses of rich es provided. The Prince had a tremen- s appetite and ate rapidly — dinner was lly over in an hour.

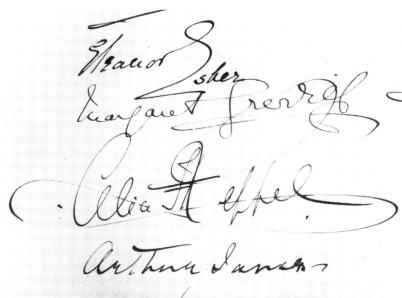

153. Four signatures in the Visitors' Book. Eleanor Esher was the wife of Lord Esher, who was one of Edward's advisers. Alice Keppel was generous, intelligent and discreet, as well as beautiful. Queen Alexandra accepted her and, when Edward was dying, brought her to his bedside. Arthur James was Willie's eldest brother.

154. Ready for the shoot, 26 November — 1 December 1894. Gamekeepers (in bowler hats), beaters and retrievers in the arboretum, ready for the shoot.

. (*below*) The Prince of Wales's signature and a record of a
·e days' shoot, in November 1896. Though he liked shooting,
t he enjoyed above all was the outdoor sport in the company
·thers as happy and relaxed as himself.

. (*right*) Shooting in West Dean Park. The marksman has
·wn loader, as well as a keeper's boy to carry the bag for the
·ridges.

November 10

Albert Edward &c.

BEAT	Pheasants	Part-ridges	Hares	Rabbits	Wood-cock	Various	TOTAL
West Dean Wood	1044		7	55	3		1109
Arboretum	1262		40	35			1337
Highdown	704	7	45	39			795
TOTAL	3010	7	92	129	3		3241

Alfonso R H.

13ᵗ *nov.* 1907

November 11ᵗ — 16ᵗ.

Grove

King Alfonso of Spain with three attendants — two to
·ry the spent cartridges and reload, and one to carry his
·ting stick. His royal retinue at West Dean Park included
·Marques de Villalobar and the Duque de Alba.

158.   King Alfonso's signature.

(*overleaf*) Shooting party, 26 November — 1 December, 1894; Mrs. James is in the back row, second from the right,
·Willie James is sitting, third from the right. The old cottage, just below the Norwegian hut in the arboretum, was pulled
·n in 1908.

160. (*opposite above*) Ready for a ride in the governess cart, October 1894; Mrs. James with one of her four daughters and Willie James (centre). The cart was entered from behind, by a step. This was easier and safer for small children, as it kept them well away from the pony's hooves.

161. (*opposite below*) Guests from West Dean Park at Goodwood, 25-30 July 1898. The beech trees, much loved by Princess Alexandra, came right up to the course. They had not yet been cut down to make way for a new stand.

162. (*above*) The wagonette. The job of the boy on the tail-ladder was to open the back door and lower the steps. (He is probably Alan Oliver, the lodge-keeper's son.) Willie James (1854-1912) is on the left. He is remembered by an estate worker as a man of authority, business-like and straightforward.

163. (*overleaf*) An afternoon under the trees, July 1894. Mrs. James is on the right, and in the background the men are playing croquet. West Dean Park has always been known for the great variety of its trees and shrubs.

WEST DEAN PARK CHICHESTER, AND THE INFANT HEIR.

PRESENTATION

OF GOLD PLATE

For the Son and Heir,

CONSISTING OF

Plate, Bowl, Knife, Fork and Spoon,
Serviette Ring, Egg Cup and Spoon, and
Mug.

Signal Maroon will announce departure of
carriage from Station.

TORCHLIGHT PROCESSION

HEADED BY

The Chichester Prize Brass Band

(Under Bandmaster Bottrill).

March   ...   " Welcome Home "   ... *C. W. Hewitt.*
(Introducing " Home Sweet Home.")

The Drive to West Dean House will be
illuminated with thousands of coloured
VENETIAN LAMPS.

During the Procession COLOURED FIRES
will be burnt in the Grounds.

164 & 165. (*opposite*) The birth of Edward James in 1907 was an occasion for great rejoicing. A postcard was made of ⁓e photograph (*top*) and a booklet printed about the celebrations at West Dean Park. After the official 'Reception of ⁓. and Mrs. William James at Singleton Station at 6.17 p.m.' The committee presented a sincerely respectful address, ⁓well as a set 'of Gold Plate for the Son and Heir.' The festivities later included a spectacular display of fireworks.

⁓6. (*above*) Edward James in the tapestried Oak Hall. Educated at Eton and Oxford, he became a poet, author and ⁓ron of the arts, and particularly of painters of the surrealist movement. Today he lives in Mexico. At West Dean ⁓k he has endowed a charitable educational trust to keep alive traditional crafts, to which in 1964 he conveyed most ⁓the estates, some of whose fields are now the Weald and Downland Open Air Museum.

7. (*opposite above*) Outside West Dean shop, ⸺ut the turn of the century. Mrs. Court (on the ⸺ht) who started it here, lived to be 95. With her ⸺ Mr. and Mrs. Napper, and (standing) Mrs. Pannell ⸺ the shop assistant.

⸺. (*opposite below*) Here is West Dean shop at ⸺ beginning of World War 2. Left to right: Anne ⸺ller, the owner's daughter; Ern Boxall, who baked ⸺ad and cakes at the back; Mrs. Kathleen Bryce, ⸺tmistress; Florrie Standing and another assistant; ⸺ and Mrs. Moller, the owners.

⸺. (*right*) George Penny, Singleton shepherd, ⸺ two new-born lambs, in December 1974. ⸺ning from a family of well-known shepherds, ⸺ has exported ewes, ewe lambs and rams to ⸺nce, as well as winning numerous prizes at ⸺ling shows all over the U.K. His flock of 200 ⸺s was the only Dorset Down flock ever to win ⸺ breed championship at the Royal Agricultural ⸺w at Kenilworth three years in succession.

⸺. (*below*) Jack Daniel and H. P. Renwick, ⸺ws Hall Farm, 1945.

. (*opposite above*) In *The Selsey
ns*, West Dean, at the beginning
World War 2. (Left) Mr. Roberts,
publican, who used to be a fast
vler in the Sussex Cricket XI,
h his daughter Joan Nicklin and
stomer.

. (*opposite below*) Keith Phillips;
Algy and George Lillywhite, sawing, timber and pulpwood mer-
nts. They are felling diseased elms
ingleton by the river, in October
4. The spread of Dutch elm disease
sadly affected the whole country,
our valley has not been spared.

. (*right*) Roger Champion, master
tsman, at work pegging the timber
e of Pendean Farmhouse, at the
ld and Downland Open Air
eum, Singleton. The main pur-
 of the Museum is to rescue
d domestic buildings in the South
 of England that are threatened
h destruction and to encourage
lic interest in them. It also
vides a growing educational
ice and depends very largely on
nteer help.

(*below*) The completed Pendean
nhouse.

175. Two Andrews in a tub, with a white poodle and a parrot, on Singleton pond in the 1960s.